Table of Cont

Jnit 1 Birthdays	page 2
Jnit 2 The Great Outdoors	page 10
Jnits 1–2 Listen and Review	page 18
Let's Read About Chris and Cindy's Treasure Hunt Part One	page 19
Jnit 3 Hopes and Dreams	page 20
Jnit 4 School	page 28
Jnits 3–4 Listen and Review	page 36
Let's Read About Chris and Cindy's Treasure Hunt Part Two	page 37
Unit 5 Indoors and Outdoors	page 38
Unit 6 People	page 44
Units 5–6 Listen and Review	page 54
Let's Read About Chris and Cindy's Treasure Hunt Part Three	page 55
Unit 7 Future Plans	page 56
Unit 8 Work and Play	page 64
Units 7–8 Listen and Review	page 72
Let's Read About Chris and Cindy's Treasure Hunt Part Four	page 73
Syllabus	page 74
Word List	page 77

Let's Start

Let's Learn More

Let's Build

Let's Read

Units Review

Let's Read About

Unit 1 Birthdays

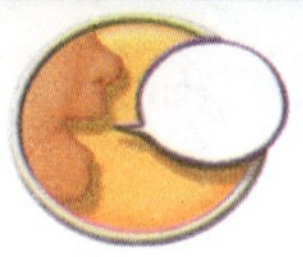

Let's Start

A. Let's talk.

B. Let's practice.

When's your birthday?
It's on August 3rd.

C. Practice the sentences. Ask and answer.

What's the date today?
It's the 21st.
What was the date yesterday?
It was the 20th.
What's the date going to be tomorrow?
It's going to be the 22nd.

January

Sunday	Monday	Tuesday	Wednesday	Thursday	Friday	Saturday
1 1st	2 2nd	3 3rd	4 4th	5 5th	6 6th	7 7th
8 8th	9 9th	10 10th	11 11th	12 12th	13 13th	14 14th
15 15th	16 16th	17 17th	18 18th	19 19th	20 20th	21 Today! 21st
22 22nd	23 23rd	24 24th	25 25th	26 26th	27 27th	28 28th
29 29nd	30 30th	31 31st				

February

S	M	T	W	T	F	S
			1	2	3	4
5	6	7	8	9	10	11
12	13	14	15	16	17	18
19	20	21	22	23	24	25
26	27	28				

March

S	M	T	W	T	F	S
			1	2	3	4
5	6	7	8	10	10	11
12	13	14	15	16	17	18
19	20	21	22	23	24	25
26	27	28	29	30	31	

April

S	M	T	W	T	F	S
						1
2	3	4	5	6	7	8
9	10	11	12	13	14	15
16	17	18	19	20	21	22
23/30	24	25	26	27	28	29

May

S	M	T	W	T	F	S
	1	2	3	4	5	6
7	8	10	10	11	12	13
14	15	16	17	18	19	20
21	22	23	24	25	26	27
28	29	30	31			

June

S	M	T	W	T	F	S
				1	2	3
4	5	6	7	8	9	10
11	12	13	14	15	16	17
18	19	20	21	22	23	24
25	26	27	28	29	30	

July

S	M	T	W	T	F	S
						1
2	3	4	5	6	7	8
9	10	11	12	13	14	15
16	19	20	21	22	23	24
25	26	27	28	29	30	31

August

S	M	T	W	T	F	S
1	2	3	4	5	6	7
8	9	10	11	12	12	14
15	16	17	18	19	20	21
22	23	24	25	26	27	28
29	30	31				

September

S	M	T	W	T	F	S
			1	2	3	4
5	6	7	8	9	10	11
12	13	14	15	16	17	18
19	20	21	22	23	24	25
26	27	28	29	30		

October

S	M	T	W	T	F	S
					1	2
3	4	5	6	7	8	9
10	11	12	13	14	15	16
17	18	19	20	21	22	23
24/31	25	26	27	28	29	30

November

S	M	T	W	T	F	S
	1	2	3	4	5	6
7	8	9	10	11	12	13
14	15	16	17	18	19	20
21	22	23	24	25	26	27
28	29	30				

December

S	M	T	W	T	F	S
			1	2	3	4
5	6	7	8	9	10	11
12	13	14	15	16	17	18
19	20	21	22	23	24	25
26	27	28	29	30	31	

Did You Know?

What's the date?
It's the 15th.
It's May 15th.
It's Monday, May 15th.

What did he do yesterday?
He flew a kite.

Let's Learn

A. Practice the words.

1. took a test

2. had a party

3. flew a kite

4. went to the store

5. met a movie star

6. drank hot chocolate

B. Practice the sentences.

CD 1 09

He She	had a party yesterday.
He She	didn't drink hot chocolate yesterday.

take	→	took
have	→	had
fly	→	flew
go	→	went
meet	→	met
drink	→	drank

1. 2. 3. 4. 5. 6.

C. Practice the question and answer.

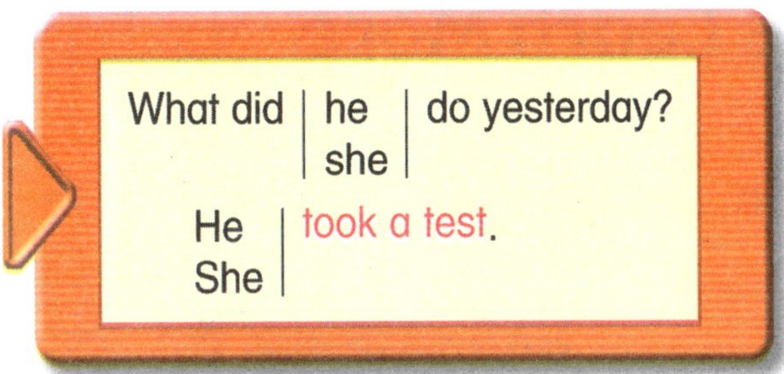

What did	he she	do yesterday?
He She	took a test.	

D. Ask and answer.

Did	he she	fly a kite yesterday?

Yes,	he she	did.	No,	he she	didn't.

He ate too much chocolate.

A. Practice the words.

1. ate too much chocolate

2. broke a window

3. got a present

4. found some money

5. lost his cell phone

6. won a race

B. Practice the sentences.

He She They	won a race.
He She They	didn't find any money.

eat	→	ate
break	→	broke
get	→	got
find	→	found
lose	→	lost
win	→	won

1\.

2\.

3\.

C. Practice the question and answer.

What happened?	He She They	found some money.

D. Practice the grammar chant.

When's your birthday?
  It was the day before yesterday.
What did you do?
  I had a party.
What happened?
  We had a race.
Did you win?
  Yes, I won. I came in 1st place!

Let's Build

A. Make sentences.

I met a movie star on the 13th.

August

S	M	T	W	T	F	S
		1	2	3	4	5
6	7	8	9	10	11	12
13	14	15	16	17	18	19
20	21	22	23	24	25	26
27	28	29	30	31		

1. lost my music player
2. found my music player
3. met a movie star
4. ate at a restaurant
5. flew a kite
6. had a party

B. Ask and answer.

When did he fly a kite?
He flew a kite on Sunday the 20th.

Let's Read

A. Read.

Welcome to Abby's Page

My birthday was great this year. First, my parents and I went to a restaurant for breakfast. I had birthday candles on my pancakes! Then, we went to the Space Center. I took a tour and met an astronaut. It was a lot of fun!

B. Answer the questions.

1. How was Abby's birthday this year?
2. Did she eat breakfast at home?
3. Who did she meet at the Space Center?

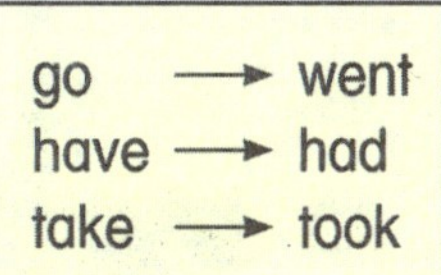

go	→	went
have	→	had
take	→	took

New Words

parents
candles
Space Center
tour
astronaut

C. Choose the sentence with the same meaning.

My parents and I went to the Space Center.

1. I went to the Space Center.
2. We went to the Space Center.
3. They went to the Space Center.

Unit 2 The Great Outdoors

Let's Start

A. Let's talk.

B. Let's practice.

The school trip is tomorrow. I'm really excited!
Me, too!

C. Practice the words. Ask and answer.

1. cool

2. cold

3. warm

4. hot

5. foggy

6. humid

What's the weather going to be like tomorrow?
It's going to be cold.

D. Practice the grammar chant.

What's the weather going to be like tomorrow?
The newspaper says it's going to snow.
Do you think we should take our umbrellas?
I'm not the weatherman. I don't know!

Should he take a towel?

Yes, he should.

Let's Learn

A. Practice the words.

CD 1
28

1. a towel

2. a hat

3. a swimsuit

4. a tent

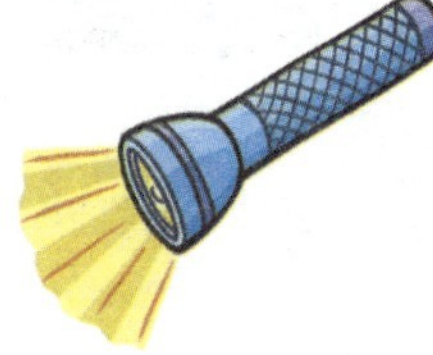

5. a flashlight

6. a sleeping bag

7. sunglasses

8. sunscreen

B. Say these. CD 1 29

He's going to go to the mountains.

She's going to go to the beach.

C. Practice the sentences.

CD 1
30

CD 1
31

He She	should take sunscreen.	He She	shouldn't take a tent.

D. Practice the question and answer.

Should	he she they	take sunscreen?

Yes,	he she they	should.	No,	he she they	shouldn't.

shouldn't = should not

1.

2.

3.

4.

5.

a.

b.

c.

d.

e.

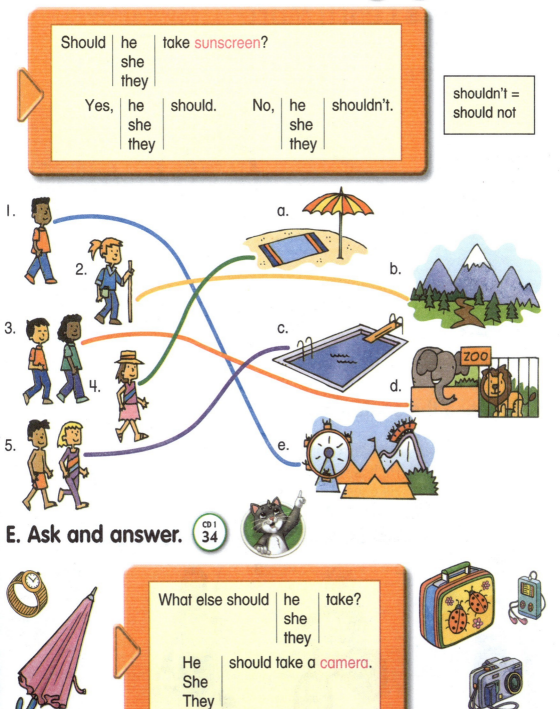

E. Ask and answer.

CD 1 34

What else should	he she they	take?

He She They	should take a camera.

What's she going to do?

She's probably going to play tennis.

Let's Learn More

A. Practice the words.

1. a mitt

2. a bat

3. a bicycle

4. a helmet

5. a tennis ball

6. a tennis racket

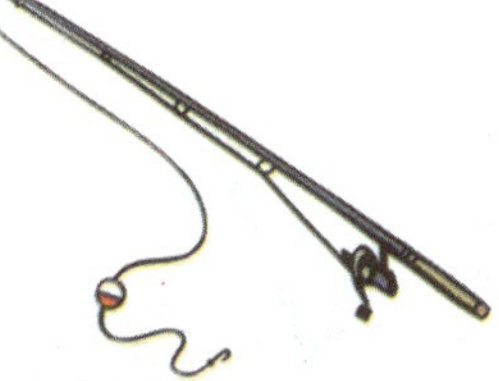
7. a fishing rod

8. a bucket

B. Practice the sentences.

He has a mitt and a bat.
He doesn't have a fishing rod or a bucket.
He's probably going to play baseball.

1.

2.

3.

4.

C. Practice the question and answer. 

What's | he / she | going to do?

He's / She's | probably going to go hiking.

What are they going to do?

They're probably going to play baseball.

play baseball
play tennis
ride a bicycle
go fishing
go hiking
go swimming

1. 

2. 

3. 

4. 

5. 

6. 

He's going to eat. = 100% sure
He's probably going to eat. = not 100% sure

Let's Build

A. Make sentences.

He has a towel. He's probably going to go to the pool.
She wants a cat. She's probably going to go to the pet store.
They have a kite. They're probably going to go to the park.

B. Ask and answer.

Where's he / she going to go?

He's / She's probably going to go to the library.

Where are they going to go?

They're probably going to go to the park.

Let's Read

A. Read.

How to Make a Rainbow

Do you like rainbows? You can make a rainbow indoors.

First, put water in a glass.

Second, put a small mirror inside the glass and tilt it up slightly.

Third, turn off the lights.

Shine a flashlight onto the mirror. You're going to see a rainbow on the wall!

New Words

a rainbow	tilt it up slightly
indoors	turn off the lights
mirror	shine

B. Answer the questions.

1. Can you make a rainbow?
2. What should you do first?
3. Where are you going to see a rainbow?

C. Choose the correct picture.

Which picture shows the meaning of *tilt it up slightly*?

a.

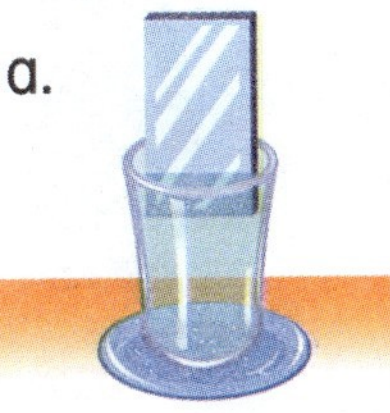

b.

c.

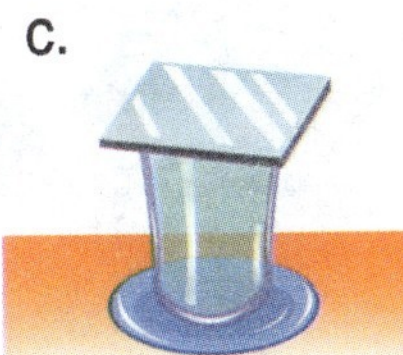

Units 1-2 Listen and Review

A. Listen and write.

SUNDAY	MONDAY	TUESDAY	WEDNESDAY	THURSDAY	FRIDAY	SATURDAY
____	TODAY 18th	____	____	____	____	____

B. Listen and circle.

1. a b c
2. a b c
3. a b c
4. a b c
5. a b c
6. a b c

Let's Read About

CHRIS AND CINDY'S TREASURE HUNT

Part One

A. Read.

"We're going to go on a treasure hunt," said Aunt Angie. "We're going to take my airplane."

"Yeah!" said Chris and Cindy.

Aunt Angie had the first clue for the treasure hunt. Chris and Cindy read it.

New Words

- treasure hunt
- clue
- sand
- holding

It's not a beach, but there's a lot of sand. You should take your hats and sunscreen. Uncle Al is holding your next clue in front of a big triangle.

"I think I know!" said Cindy.

B. Where are they going to go next?

a. 

b. 

c. 

Unit 3 Hopes and Dreams

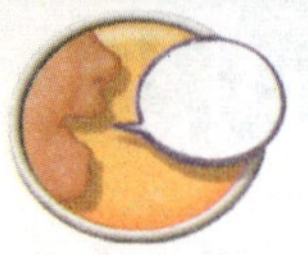

Let's Start

A. Let's talk.

CD 1 46

B. Let's practice.

CD 1 47

What do you want to be?
I want to be an astronaut.

C. Practice the words. Ask and answer.  

1. an astronaut

2. a singer

3. a musician

4. a news reporter

5. a writer

6. a scientist

Do you want to be a singer?	Yes, I do. No, I don't.

D. Practice the grammar chant. 

What do you want to be?
I want to be a dancer.
What about you?
I want to be a singer.
Great idea!
Come on, let's go.
We can sing and dance
on a TV show!

Does he want to be a pop idol?

Yes, he does.

Let's Learn

A. Practice the words.

1. a flight attendant

2. a pop idol

3. a truck driver

4. an architect

5. a tour guide

6. a delivery person

B. Practice the sentences.

He She	wants to be a flight attendant.
He She	doesn't want to be a delivery person.

1\.

2\.

3\.

C. Practice the question and answer.

What does	he she	want to be?	He She	wants to be a truck driver.

D. Ask and answer.

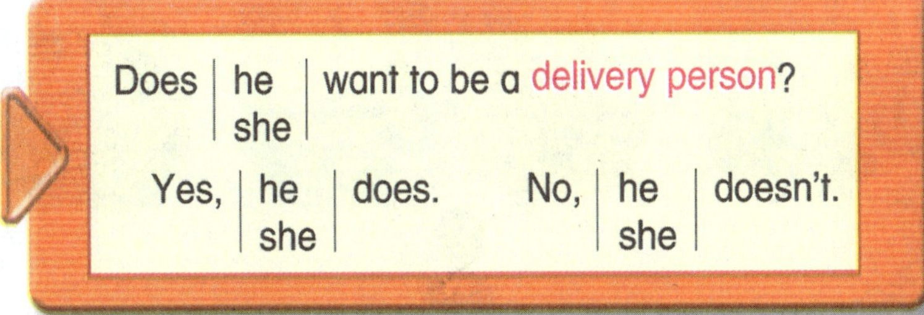

Does	he she	want to be a delivery person?

Yes,	he she	does.	No,	he she	doesn't.

What does she want to do?

She wants to sail a boat.

Let's Learn More

A. Practice the words.

CD 1 57

1. climb a mountain

2. build a house

3. sail a boat

4. travel around the world

5. design a video game

6. drive a car

B. Practice the sentences.

He She	wants to drive a car.
He She	doesn't want to travel around the world.

1.

2.

3.

C. Practice the question and answer.

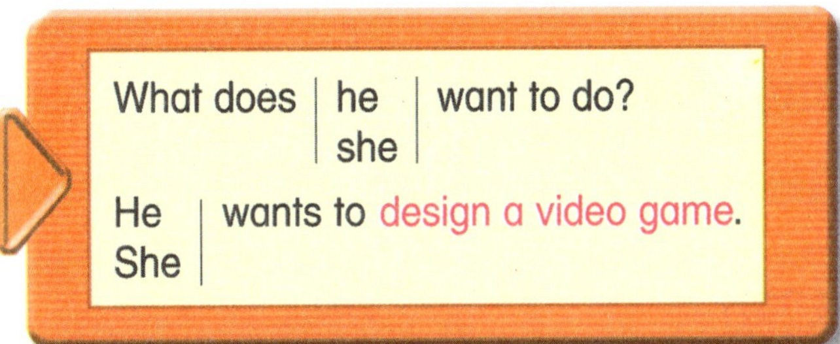

What does	he she	want to do?
He She	wants to design a video game.	

D. Ask and answer.

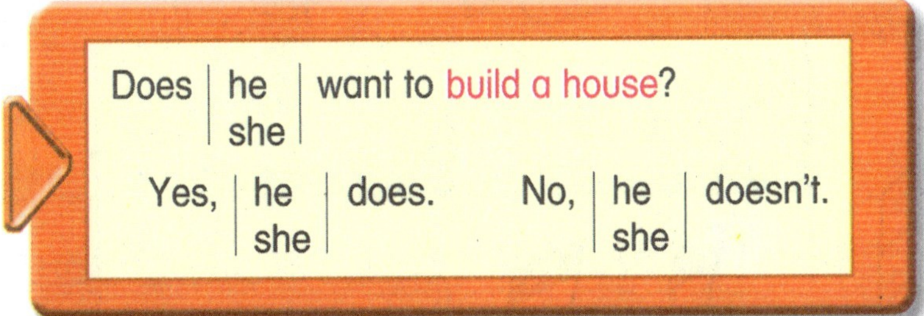

Does	he she	want to build a house?

Yes,	he she	does.	No,	he she	doesn't.

E. What about you?

What do you want to do?

Let's Build

Play the game. Make sentences.

I want to ____________, but I don't want to ____________.

Start

- study English / speak English
- talk on the telephone / watch TV
- swim / run
- play Ping-Pong / play baseball
- use chopsticks / do a magic trick
- ride a bicycle / drive a car
- walk the dog / feed the turtle
- sing / dance
- eat an apple / drink hot chocolate
- do homework / listen to music
- cook dinner / make breakfast
- take pictures / take a bath

Finish

Let's Read

A. Read.

Anna and Teri Johnson, Volunteer Sisters

Anna Johnson is a volunteer at the zoo. She likes to work with animals. She works with dolphins every day. She feeds them every morning and helps train them, too. Someday Anna wants to be a dolphin trainer.

Teri is Anna's sister. She is a volunteer at the hospital. She doesn't want to work with animals. She likes to help people. She wants to be a nurse someday.

New Words

volunteer trainer
dolphins hospital

B. Answer the questions.

1. What is Anna doing at the zoo?
2. Does she like to work with animals?
3. What does Teri want to be?

C. Choose the correct answer.

What does a dolphin trainer do?

a. rides on a train with dolphins
b. drives a train with dolphins
c. works with dolphins

Let's Start

A. Let's talk.

B. Let's practice.

Why do you like science?
I think it's easy.

C. Practice the words. Ask and answer.  

1. history

2. science

3. English

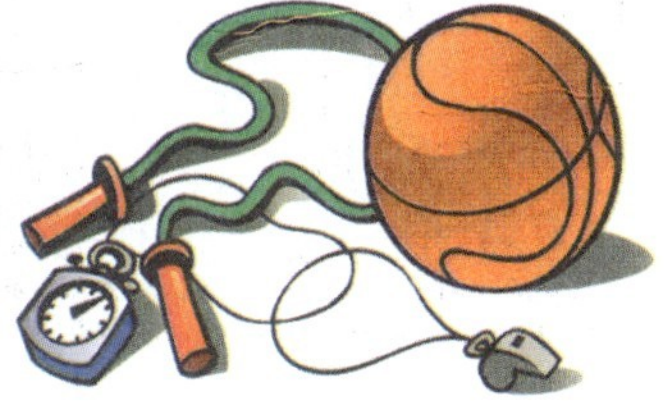

4. P.E. (physical education)

5. geography

6. literature

What's your favorite subject?
I like history.

D. Practice the grammar chant. 

What's your favorite subject?
I like P.E.
Why do you like it?
No homework!
What about you?
I like science.
Why do you like it?
Nice teacher!

E. What about you?

What's your favorite subject?

Let's Learn

Which poster is the biggest?

The blue poster is the biggest.

A. Practice the words.

1\.

bottle / bottles

2\.

box / boxes

3\.

bag / bags

B. Practice the sentences.

The orange bottle is bigger than the blue bottle.
The green bottle is the biggest.

big

bigger

biggest

small

smaller

smallest

C. Practice the questions and answers.

Which pencil is the longest?
The yellow pencil is the longest.
Which pencil is the shortest?
The red pencil is the shortest.

big	→	bigger	→	the biggest
small	→	smaller	→	the smallest
long	→	longer	→	the longest
short	→	shorter	→	the shortest
heavy	→	heavier	→	the heaviest
light	→	lighter	→	the lightest

1. heavy / light

2. long / short

3. big / small

4. light / heavy

5. short / long

6. small / big

D. Ask and answer.

Is the blue pencil the longest?
Yes, it is. No, it isn't.

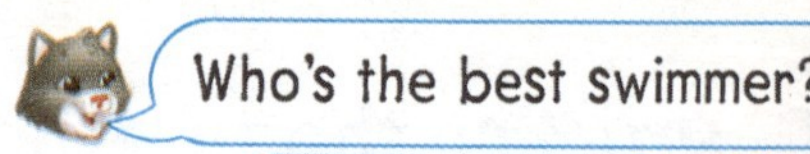

Who's the best swimmer?

Let's Learn More

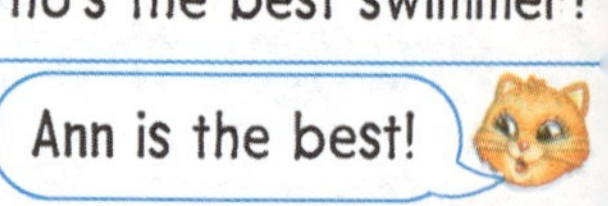

Ann is the best!

A. Practice the words.

B. Practice the sentence.

Matt's pie is good.

C. Practice the questions and answers.

Who's the	best worst	swimmer?	Ryan is the best. Kevin is the worst.

 = Ryan

 = Ann

 = Kevin

1. swimmer

2. dancer

3. singer

4. runner

5. soccer player

6. cook

D. Ask and answer.

Is Kevin a better runner than Ann?
Yes, he is. No, he isn't.

Is Kevin the best swimmer?
Yes, he is. No, he isn't.

Let's Build

A. Make sentences.

The police car is heavier than the motorcycle.
The fire engine is the heaviest.

heavy

light

big

long

1. motorcycle
   police car
   fire engine
2. paper
   pencil
   paper clip
3. hairbrush
   key
   coin
4. ruler
   jump rope
   ribbon

B. Practice the grammar chant.

CD 1
84

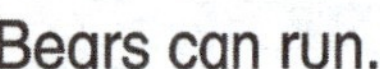

Bears can run.
Lions run faster.
But cheetahs are the fastest of them all!

Don't ever race with a cheetah.
Cheetahs are the fastest of them all!

Rhinos are big.
Polar bears are bigger.
But elephants are the biggest of them all!

Don't ever fight with an elephant.
Elephants are the biggest of them all!

Let's Read

A. Read.

Which One Is the Fastest?

Some animals are fast and some are slow. Some animals move only on land and some move only in water. Other animals move in the air. Let's look at the speed of some animals.

1. Which animal is the fastest on land?

a. a lion

b. a cheetah

c. a horse

2. Which animal is the fastest in the air?

a. a swan

b. a duck

c. a falcon

3. Which animal is the fastest in water?

a. a sailfish

b. a dolphin

c. a whale

Animal	Speed (kph)
falcon	320
swan	90
duck	85
cheetah	112
lion	80
horse	76
sailfish	109
whale	54
dolphin	40

New Words

on land, in water, in the air, swan, falcon, sailfish, whale

Answers to Quiz: 1. b. 2. c. 3. a.

B. Do you know?

1. Which three animals are the fastest?
2. Which animal is the fastest of all?
3. Which animal is the slowest in water?

C. Choose the correct answer.

Where does a dolphin live?

1. in water 2. on water 3. by water

Units 3-4 Listen and Review

A. Listen and circle.

1.

2.

3.

4.

B. Listen and check.

1.

2.

3.

4.

Nina

Jill

John

Let's Read About

CHRIS AND CINDY'S TREASURE HUNT

Part Two

A. Read.

CD 1 88

"Egypt is hot!" said Chris.

"Look," said Cindy. "There's the Great Pyramid."

"And there's Uncle Al with three water bottles!" said Chris.

"Hi, kids!" he said.

"Hi, Uncle Al. Do you have our next clue?" asked Cindy.

"Yes, I do," he said. "Here it is."

New Words

Egypt
Great Pyramid
kids
waterfall

Find the biggest waterfall and ride a boat in front of it.

"This clue is harder," said Cindy.
"But I think I know," said Chris.

B. Where are they going to go next?

a. 

b. 

c. 

 Unit 5 Indoors and Outdoors

Let's Start

A. Let's talk. 

B. Let's practice. 

Can you wait for us?	Sure, no problem! Sorry, I can't.

C. Practice the words and sentences.  

1. worried

2. surprised

3. interested

4. excited

5. bored

6. embarrassed

He's She's	surprised.

D. Practice the grammar chant. CD 2 06

He's very worried.
So is she.
She's excited.
So are we.
We're surprised.
So are they.
Our teacher gave
a test today.

A. Practice the words.

1. watched a baseball game

2. practiced the violin

3. downloaded music

4. listened to the radio

5. played a board game

6. visited their grandparents

B. Practice the sentences.

CD 2 08

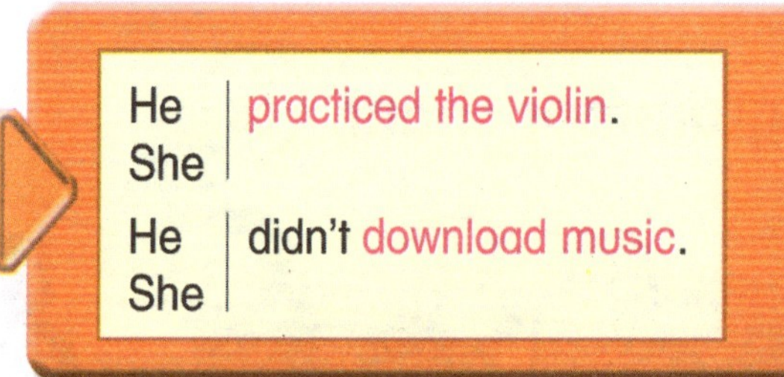

2.

3.

C. Practice the questions and answers.  

What did he / she do yesterday?	He / She practiced the violin.
What did they do yesterday?	They visited their grandparents.

1\. 

2\. 

3\. 

4\. 

D. Ask and answer.  

Did he / she listen to the radio?

Yes, he / she did. No, he / she didn't.

Did they play a board game

Yes, they did. No, they didn't.

E. What about you?

What did you do this morning? What did you do yesterday?

Let's Learn More

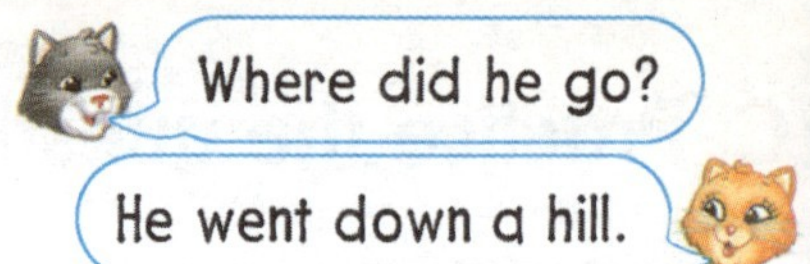

Where did he go?
He went down a hill.

A. Say these.

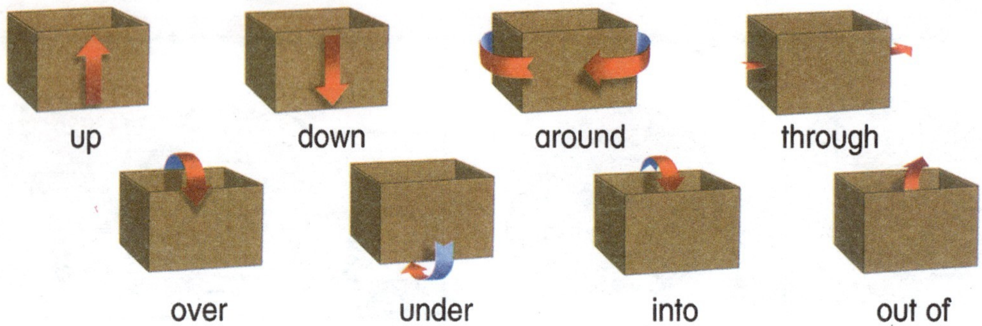

B. Practice the words.

1.

under a bridge up a hill

2.
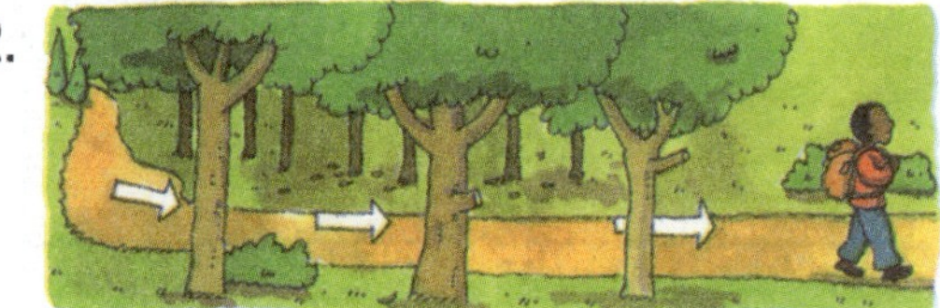

into the woods out of the woods

3.

around a pond over a bridge

4.

through a tunnel down a hill

C. Practice the sentence.

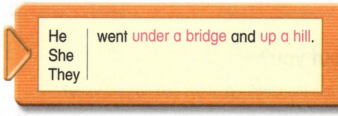

He She They	went under a bridge and up a hill.

D. Practice the question and answer.

CD 2 18

Where did the	boy girl	go?	He went over the wall. She went over the tunnel.

E. Where did the cat and dog go?

CD 2 19

Let's Build

A. Answer the questions. CD 2 20

Where did Ken go?
Who did he go with?
What did he do?
What did he eat?
When did he go?

Where did Stacy go?
Who did she go with?
What did she do?
What did she eat?
When did she go?

March 13th

February 22nd

New Words

amusement park
ride a roller coaster
french fries
museum
sandwich
look at pictures

B. What about you?

1. Where did you go for your summer vacation?
2. Who did you go with?
3. What did you do?
4. What did you eat?
5. When did you go?

Let's Read

A. Read.

Aunt Tina's Trip

Dear Joey,

We are having fun in Australia! Uncle Mark and I went to the wildlife park yesterday. I fed a kangaroo and held a koala. Uncle Mark went through the reptile house and fed a crocodile. He looked scared! Tomorrow we are going to go sailing.

See you soon!
Aunt Tina

Joey Johnson
21 Maple Road
Rockview, MN 12345

New Words

Australia
wildlife park
kangaroo
koala
reptile
crocodile

feed	→	fed
hold	→	held

B. Answer the questions.

1. Where are Aunt Tina and Uncle Mark?
2. Who fed a kangaroo?
3. Where are they going to go tomorrow?

C. Choose the correct picture.

Which picture shows the meaning of *He looked scared*?

a. 

b. 

c. 

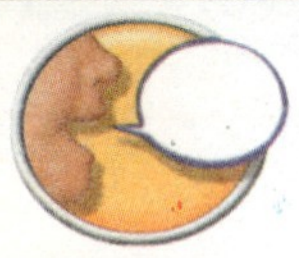

Let's Start

A. Let's talk.

CD 2 22

B. Let's practice.

CD 2 23

Can I help you?
Yes, thanks.
No, thanks. I'm OK.

Did You Know?

The word *one* in *someone* means *person* or *people.*

someone = one person
no one = no people
everyone = all people

C. Practice the words. Ask and answer.

CD 2
24

CD 2
25

Kate

1. aunt

2. uncle

3. cousin

4. younger sister

5. mom

6. dad

7. grandma

8. grandpa

Who are you looking for?
I'm looking for my aunt.

mom = mother
dad = father
grandma = grandmother
grandpa = grandfather

D. Practice the grammar chant.

CD 2 26

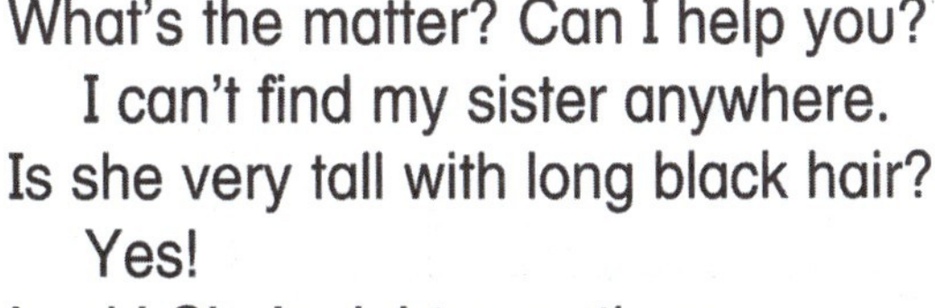

What's the matter? Can I help you?
I can't find my sister anywhere.
Is she very tall with long black hair?
Yes!
Look! She's right over there.
That's my sister. What a surprise.
Long black hair and beautiful eyes!

Let's Learn

A. Practice the words.

Hair Color
brown hair
black hair
blond hair
red hair
gray hair

Hair Style
curly hair
long hair
straight hair
a pony tail
bangs

Face
a moustache
a beard

Eye Color
black eyes
brown eyes
blue eyes
green eyes

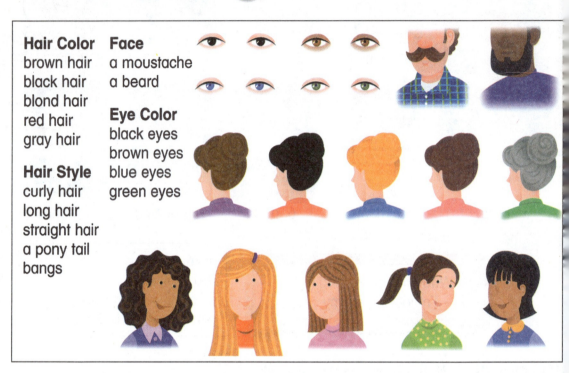

B. Practice the sentence.

He / She	has short red hair and green eyes.

C. Practice the question and answer.  

What does his cousin look like?
His cousin has brown hair and blue eyes.

1. cousin

2. friend

3. older sister

4. younger brother

5. aunt

6. uncle

7. grandma

8. grandpa

9. mom

10. dad

D. What about you?

1. What do you look like?
2. What does your cousin look like?
3. What does your friend look like?

Which girl is her cousin?

She's the girl in a red baseball cap.

Let's Learn More

A. Practice the words.

1. a vest

2. a baseball cap

3. a blouse

4. a tie

5. a suit

6. sandals

7. sneakers

8. glasses

B. Practice the sentence.

CD 2 34

I'm wearing a vest.
I'm not wearing a suit.

C. Practice the question and answer. CD 2 35 CD 2 36

Which boy is Brian's older brother?
He's the boy with curly brown hair and brown eyes.
He's the boy in shorts and a blue, striped shirt.

1. older brother
2. older sister
3. mom
4. uncle
5. dad
6. grandpa
7. aunt
8. grandma
9. younger brother

man
woman
boy
girl

D. Practice the grammar chant. CD 2 37

Is that Jim's older brother there,
the boy in shorts with the curly hair?
No, Jim's brother is wearing jeans
and a long purple T-shirt from New Orleans.

Let's Build

A. Look and answer the questions.

CD 2 38

1. Anna is the girl in the red shorts and white T-shirt.
   She's the girl with a long, black ponytail and bangs.
   Where's Anna?
2. Alex is the boy with short, curly brown hair and brown eyes.
   He's in the red sneakers and yellow T-shirt.
   Where's Alex?
3. Emily is the woman in the gray suit and white blouse.
   She's the woman with short blond hair and blue eyes.
   Where's Emily?
4. Sam is the man in the black jeans and glasses.
   He's the man with a moustache and green eyes.
   Where's Sam?

B. Answer the questions.

CD 2 39

1. What is Anna doing?
2. Who is Alex with?
3. What is Emily eating?
4. Where is Sam going to go?

Let's Read

A. Read.

Let's make a fingerprint. First, put lotion on your hands. Then, touch a mirror.

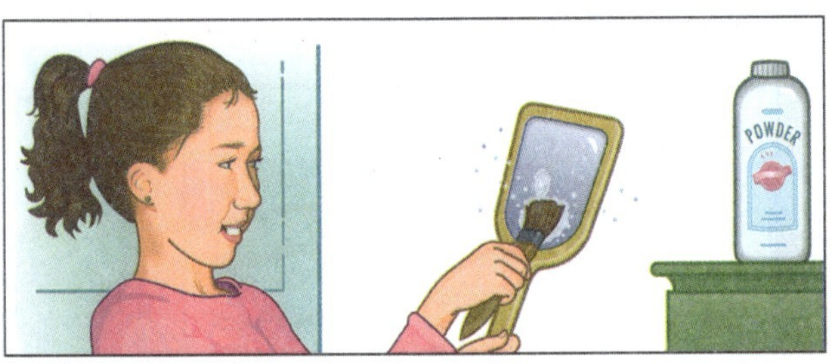

Put powder on the mirror. Brush the powder away. You should see a fingerprint.

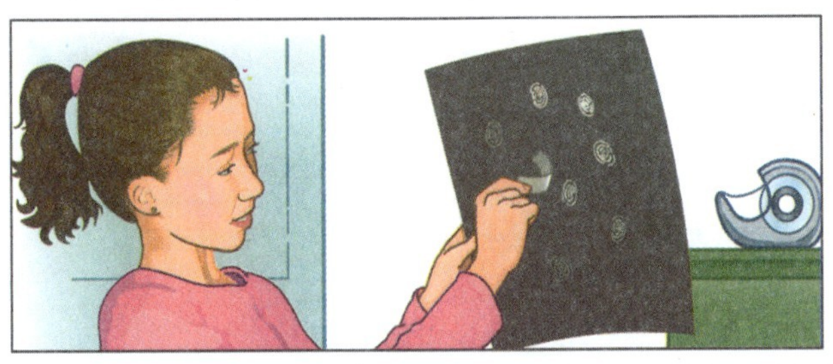

Put a piece of tape on the fingerprint. Lift the tape and put it on a piece of black paper. Do this for every finger. Then you can see all of your fingerprints. Every fingerprint is different!

New Words

fingerprint
lotion
powder
a piece of tape
lift

B. Answer the questions.

1. Where can you find your fingerprints?
2. Where do you put the powder?
3. Are all fingerprints the same?

C. Choose the best title.

1. My Fingerprint Is Different
2. You Should Look at Fingerprints
3. Let's Make Fingerprints

Units 5-6 Listen and Review

A. Listen and circle.

1.

a b c

2.

a b c

3.

4.

a b c

a b c

B. Listen and number.

CHRIS AND CINDY'S TREASURE HUNT

Part Three

A. Read.

"Iguazu Falls is beautiful!" said Cindy.

"But I'm wet!" said Chris.

"Are you Chris and Cindy?" asked a man.

"Yes, we are!"

"Here's your clue," said the man.

This place is in the desert, but it's always cold. It's underground and dark. Find your treasure near the castle in the Big Room.

New Words

Iguazu Falls
wet
desert
underground
castle
cave

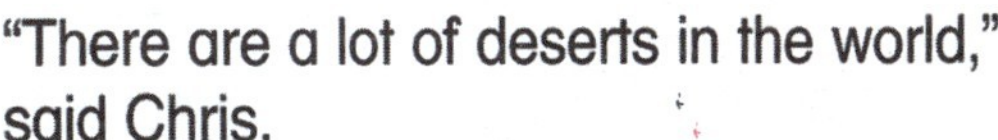

"There are a lot of deserts in the world," said Chris.

"But this is a desert with a big cave," said Cindy. "I think I know."

B. Where are they going to go next?

a. 

b. 

c. 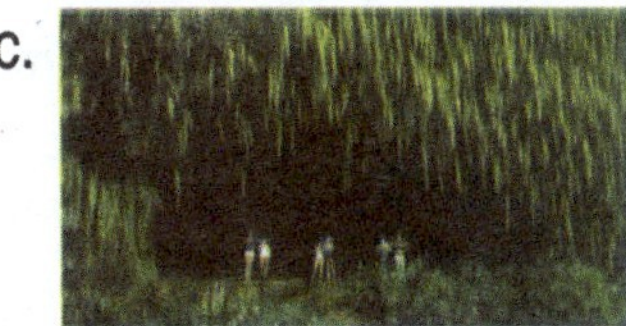

Let's Start

A. Let's talk.

B. Let's practice.

Are you going to do anything this weekend?
Yes, I am. I'm going to see my cousin.
No, I'm not. I'm going to stay home.

C. Practice the words. Ask and answer.  

1. go shopping

2. plant flowers

3. play ice hockey

4. see a play

5. go horseback riding

3. play softball

What's	he she	going to do?	He's She's	going to go shopping.
What are they going to do?			They're going to play ice hockey.	

D. Practice the grammar chant. 

What are you going to do this weekend?
    I'm going to go shopping.
What are you going to buy?
    I'm going to buy skis.
Skis? Why?
It's not going to snow.
    I know. I know.
    No mountains here. No hills, no snow.
Where are you going to ski?
    I don't know!

When's he going to go backpacking?

He's going to go backpacking in July.

Let's Learn

A. Practice the words.

1. rent a DVD tonight

2. borrow some books tomorrow

3. go backpacking in July

4. go on vacation next week

5. mail a letter this afternoon

6. read a novel this summer

B. Practice the sentence.

He's She's	going to rent a DVD tonight.

C. Practice the question and answer. 

When's	he / she	going to go backpacking?
He's / She's	going to go backpacking in July.	

1. July

2. tomorrow

3. this evening

4. next weekend

5. on Saturday

6. after school

D. Ask and answer. 

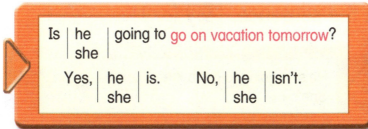

Is	he / she	going to go on vacation tomorrow?
Yes,	he / she	is.
No,	he / she	isn't.

Where's he going to go?

He's going to go to the barber shop.

Let's Learn More

A. Practice the words. 

1. department store

2. barber shop

3. beauty salon

4. supermarket

5. drug store

6. gift shop

B. Practice the sentence.  

He's She's	going to go to the department store.

C. Practice the question and answer.  

Where's he / she going to go?

He's / She's going to go to the department store.

Where are they going to go?

They're going to go to the supermarket.

D. Ask and answer.  

Is he / she going to go to the drug store?

Yes, he / she is. No, he / she isn't.

Are they going to go to the gift shop?

Yes, they are. No, they aren't.

Let's Build

A. Make sentences. CD 2 61

Amy stayed home on Sunday.
Today she is studying English.
She's going to go to art class on Friday.

Amy's week

Sunday	Monday	Tuesday	Wednesday	Thursday	Friday	Saturday
12th	13th	14th	15th	16th	17th	18th
stay home	gymnastics	TODAY! English	shopping	math class	art class	violin practice

Ben's week

Sunday	Monday	Tuesday	Wednesday	Thursday	Friday	Saturday
12th	13th	14th	15th	16th	17th	18th
play video games	soccer practice	Today! computer class	English class	soccer practice	piano practice	play with friends

B. Ask and answer. CD 2 62

When did Amy go to math class?
When is Ben going to play with his friends?

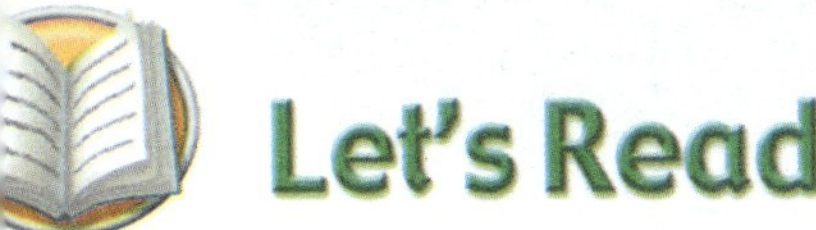

Let's Read

A. Read.

Welcome to Paul's Page!

Next summer I'm going to go on a home stay. I'm going to have an American brother and sister. Their names are Joe and Linda. Two years ago, Joe stayed with my family. Now, I'm going to stay with his family for two months. I have to study English every day!

New Words

home stay
American
for two months

B. Answer the questions.

1. When is Paul going to the United States?
2. Who stayed with Paul's family?
3. What does Paul have to do now?

C. Choose the correct answer.

What does *home stay* mean?

1. stay at home with my family
2. stay away from home
3. stay with a different family

Unit 8 Work and Play

Let's Start

A. Let's talk.

That's too bad. I hope you feel better!

Thanks. Have fun at the park.

B. Let's practice.

Do you want to come?	I can't. Sure!

C. Practice the words. Ask and answer.

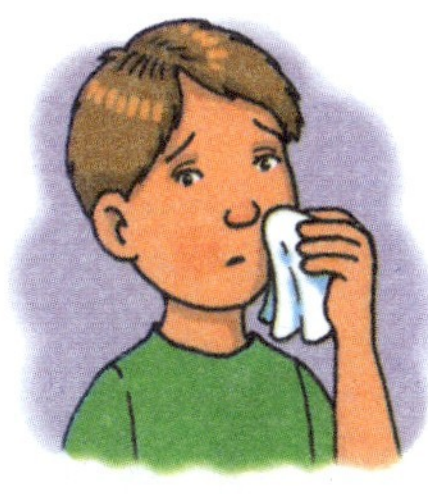
1. a cold

2. a fever

3. a headache

4. a sore throat

5. an earache

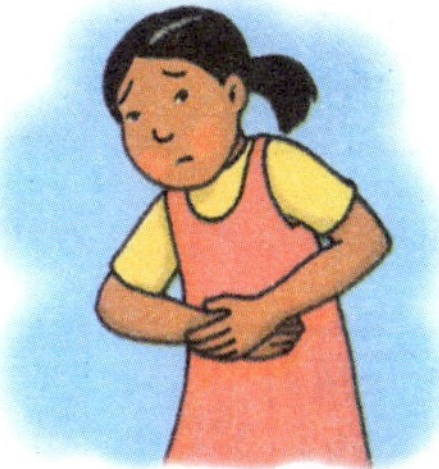
6. a stomachache

7. a toothache

8. a cough

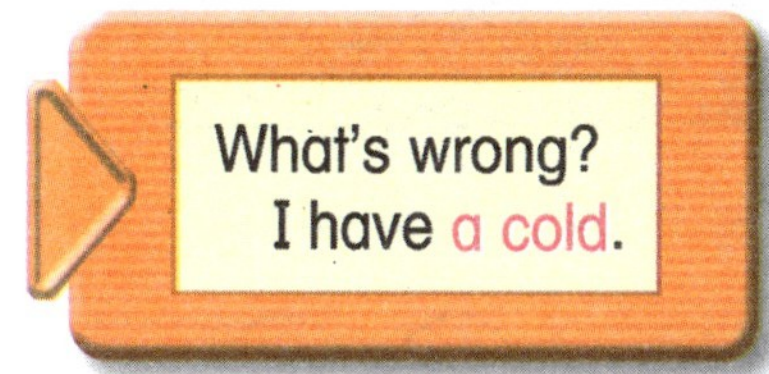

D. Practice the grammar chant.

What's the matter with you?
You don't look very well.
  I have a toothache.
Call the dentist.
  I have a stomachache.
Call the doctor.
  I have a sore throat.
Drink some tea.
  My cold is getting worse.
Call the nurse!

What does he like to do?

He likes to paint pictures.

Let's Learn

A. Practice the words. CD 2 69

1. write e-mail

2. paint pictures

3. collect baseball cards

4. watch sports on TV

5. surf the Internet

6. play badminton

B. Practice the sentences. CD 2 70 CD 2 71

He She	likes doesn't like	to write e-mail.
They	like don't like	to watch sports on TV.

1.

2.

3.

C. Practice the questions and answers. CD 2 72 CD 2 73

What does	he / she	like to do?	He / She	likes to paint pictures.
What do they like to do?			They like to play badminton.	

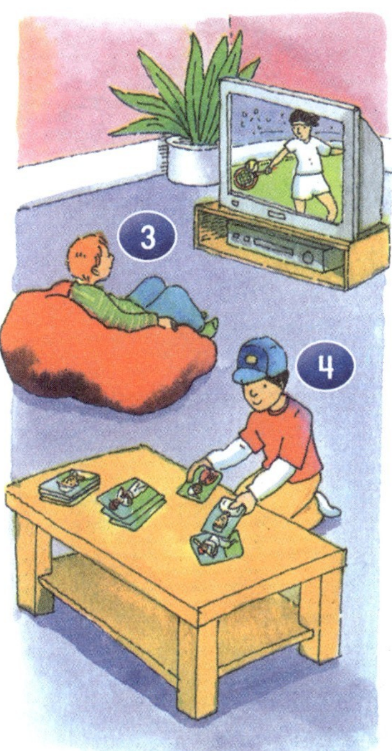

D. Ask and answer.  

CD 2 74

Does	he / she	like to collect baseball cards?			
Yes,	he / she	does.	No,	he / she	doesn't.

Do they like to watch sports on TV?

Yes, they do. No, they don't.

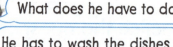

Let's Learn More

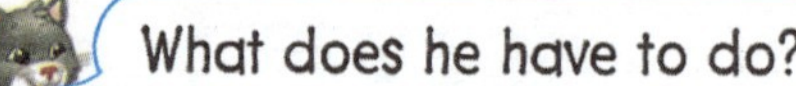
What does he have to do?
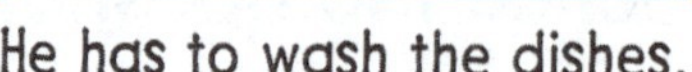
He has to wash the dishes.

A. Practice the words.

CD 2
75

1. clear the table

2. wash the dishes

3. dry the dishes

4. vacuum the carpet

5. take out the trash

6. feed the dog

B. Practice the sentences.

CD 2
76
CD 2
77

He She	has to wash the dishes.

They have to clear the table.

C. Practice the question and answer.  

What does	he she	have to do?

He She	has to take out the trash.

D. What about you?

1. What do you have to do?
2. What do you like to do?

Let's Build

Play a game. Make sentences.

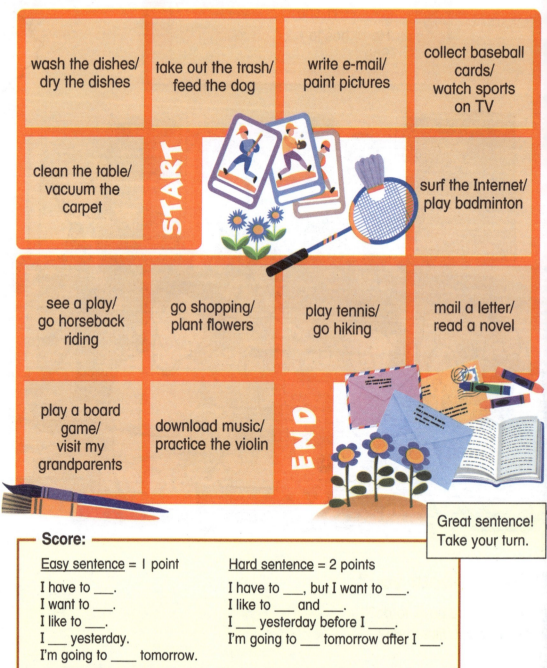

wash the dishes/ dry the dishes	take out the trash/ feed the dog	write e-mail/ paint pictures	collect baseball cards/ watch sports on TV
clean the table/ vacuum the carpet	START		surf the Internet/ play badminton
see a play/ go horseback riding	go shopping/ plant flowers	play tennis/ go hiking	mail a letter/ read a novel
play a board game/ visit my grandparents	download music/ practice the violin	END	

Great sentence! Take your turn.

Score:

Easy sentence = 1 point

I have to ___.
I want to ___.
I like to ___.
I ___ yesterday.
I'm going to ____ tomorrow.

Hard sentence = 2 points

I have to ___, but I want to ___.
I like to ___ and ___.
I ___ yesterday before I ____.
I'm going to ___ tomorrow after I ___.

Let's Read

A. Read.

What Are You Like?

1. You want to play a video game.
   You have to do your homework.
   A. I'm going to do my homework.
   B. I'm going to play a video game.

2. You have a test tomorrow.
   A. I'm going to study.
   B. I'm going to watch TV.

3. You have some money.
   A. I'm going to save it.
   B. I'm going to spend it.

Answers

All A: You are very serious. Have a little more fun!
2 A and 1 B: You are serious, but you like to have fun, too.
2 B and 1 A: You are easygoing, but you can be serious, too.
All B: You are very easygoing. Be a little more serious!

New Words

save
spend
serious
easygoing

B. What about you?

What kind of person are you? Are you a serious person or an easygoing person?

C. Choose the best answer.

Choose the best answers for the questions.

1. What are you like?
   A. I'm easygoing.
   B. I have brown hair.

2. What do you look like?
   A. I'm serious.
   B. I have blue eyes.

Units 7-8 Listen and Review

Listen and number. 

1.

2.

3.

4.

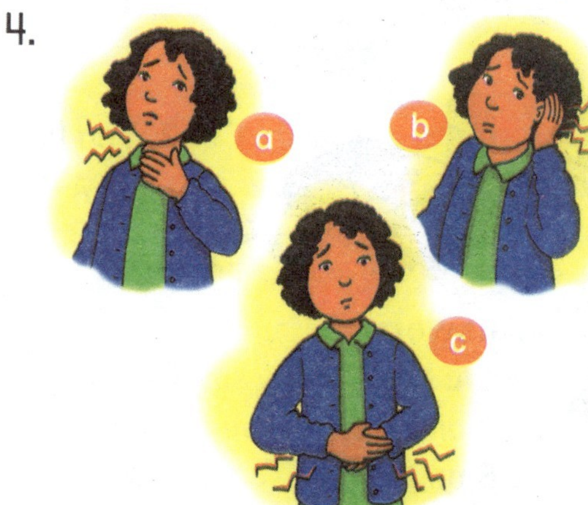

5.

6.

CHRIS AND CINDY'S TREASURE HUNT

Part Four

A. Read.

Carlsbad Caverns is so big," said Chris. "I feel so small."

"There's a box," said Cindy. "Let's look inside."

"It's a scrapbook," said Cindy.

"Look! We're riding on a camel in Egypt," said Chris.

"And we're standing in front of the waterfall at Iguazu Falls," said Cindy.

"Thank you, Aunt Angie," said Chris. "This is a great treasure."

"I'm glad you like it," said Aunt Angie.

"Why are there blank pages in the scrapbook?" asked Cindy.

"Because we're going to have more adventures!" said Aunt Angie.

B. What about you?

1. Do you have a scrapbook?
2. Where in the world do you want to go?
3. What do you want to see?

New Words

Carlsbad Caverns	blank
scrapbook	adventures
camel	

Let's Go 4 Syllabus

Unit 1 Birthdays

Let's Start	Let's Learn	Let's Learn More	Let's Build
When's your birthday? It's on August 3rd. Asking about and stating the date Asking about and stating birthdays What's the date today? It's the 21st. Asking about and stating the date	He had a party yesterday. She didn't drink hot chocolate yesterday. Stating what someone did or did not do What did he do yesterday? He took a test. Did she fly a kite yesterday? Yes, she did. No, she didn't. Asking questions with simple past irregular verbs Asking what someone did	He/She/They won a race. He/She/They didn't find any money. What happened? He/She/They found some money. Asking about and stating what happened	I met a movie star on the 13th. When did he fly a kite? He flew a kite on Sunday the 20th. Asking about and answering what happened and when **Let's Read** Welcome to Abby's Page

Unit 2 The Great Outdoors

Let's Start	Let's Learn	Let's Learn More	Let's Build
The school trip is tomorrow. I'm really excited! Me, too! Talking about what is going to happen What's the weather going to be like tomorrow? It's going to be cold. Talking about what the weather is going to be like	He's going to go to the mountains. She's going to go to the beach. Talking about where people are going to go He should take sunscreen. He shouldn't take a tent. Should he/she/they take sunscreen? Yes, he/she/they should. No, he/she//they shouldn't. What else should he/she/they take? He/She/They should take a camera. Asking for and giving advice	He has a mitt and a bat. He doesn't have a fishing rod or a bucket. He's probably going to play baseball. What's she going to do? She's probably going to go hiking. What are they going to do? They're probably going to play baseball. Asking and stating what someone may do	He has sunscreen. He's probably going to go to the beach. She wants a cat. She's probably going to go to the pet store. They have a kite. They're probably going to go to the park. Where's she going to go? She's probably going to go to the library. Where are they going to go? They're probably going to go to the park. Asking and stating where someone may go **Let's Read** How to Make a Rainbow

Units 1–2 Listen and Review — **Let's Read About Chris and Cindy Part One**

Unit 3 Hopes and Dreams

Let's Start	Let's Learn	Let's Learn More	Let's Build
What do you want to be? I want to be an astronaut. Do you want to be a singer? Yes, I do. / No, I don't. Asking about future professions	He/She wants to be a flight attendant. He/She doesn't want to be a delivery person. What does he/she want to be? He/She wants to be a truck driver. Does he/she want to be a delivery person? Yes, he/she does. No, he/she doesn't. Asking about and stating and stating future professions	He/She wants to climb a mountain. He/She doesn't want to build a house. What does he/she want to do? He/She wants to design a video game. Does she want to build a house? Yes, she does. No, she doesn't. Asking about and expressing desires	I want to ___, but I don't want to _____. Expressing desires **Let's Read** Anna and Teri Johnson, Volunteer Sisters

Unit 4 School

Let's Start	Let's Learn	Let's Learn More	Let's Build
Why do you like science? I think it's easy. What's your favorite subject? I like history. Eliciting and expressing personal opinions Comparing school subjects	The orange bottle is bigger than the blue bottle. The green bottle is the biggest. Which pencil is the longest? The yellow pencil is the longest. Which pencil is the shortest? The red pencil is the shortest. Is the green pencil the longest? Yes, it is. / No, it isn't. Comparing objects that are alike	Matt's pie is good. Who's the best /worst swimmer? Ryan is the best. Kevin is the worst. Is Kevin a better runner than Ann? Yes, he is. / No, he isn't. Is Kevin the best swimmer? Yes, he is. / No, he isn't. Comparing abilities	The police car is heavier than the motorcycle. The fire engine is the heaviest. Comparing objects that are not alike **Let's Read** Which One Is the Fastest?

Units 3–4 Listen and Review — Let's Read About Chris and Cindy Part Two

Unit 5 Indoors and Outdoors

Let's Start	Let's Learn	Let's Learn More	Let's Build
Can you wait for us? Sure, no problem! Sorry, I can't. Requesting that someone wait He's/She's surprised. Describing people's feelings	He/She practiced the violin. He/She didn't download music. What did he do yesterday? He practiced the violin. What did they do yesterday? They visited their grandparents. Did he listen to the radio? Yes, he did. No, he didn't. Did they play a board game? Yes, they did. No, they didn't. Asking and stating what someone did	He/She/They went under a bridge and up a hill. Where did the boy/girl go? He went over the wall. She went through the tunnel. Describing where people went	Where did Ken/Stacy go? Who did he/she go with? What did he/she do? What did he/she eat? When did he/she go? Answering questions with details **Let's Read** Aunt Tina's Trip

Unit 6 People			
Let's Start Can I help you? Yes, thanks. No, thanks. I'm OK. Offering someone help Who are you looking for? I'm looking for my aunt. Identifying family members	**Let's Learn** He has short red hair and green eyes. What does his cousin look like? His cousin has brown hair and blue eyes. Describing people's eye color, hair color, and hair style	**Let's Learn More** The boy is wearing glasses. Which boy is Brian's older brother? He's the boy with curly brown hair and brown eyes. He's the boy in shorts and a blue, striped shirt. Identifying people by appearance	**Let's Build** Identifying people by appearance **Let's Read** Let's Make Fingerprints
Units 5–6 Listen and Review		**Let's Read About Chris and Cindy Part Three**	
Unit 7 Future Plans			
Let's Start Are you going to do anything this weekend? Yes, I am. I'm going to see my cousin. No, I'm not. I'm going to stay home. What's he/she going to do? He's/She's going to go shopping. What are they going to do? They're going to play ice hockey. Asking and stating what people are going to do	**Let's Learn** He's going to rent a DVD tonight. When's he/she going to go backpacking? He's/She's going to go backpacking in July. Is he going to go on vacation tomorrow? Yes, he is. No, he isn't. Asking and stating what people are going to do and when	**Let's Learn More** He's going to go to the department store. Where's he going to go? He's going to go to the department store. Where are they going to go? They're going to go to the supermarket. Is he going to go to the drug store? Yes, he is. / No, he isn't. Are they going to go to the gift shop? Yes, they are. / No, they aren't. Asking and answering about where someone is going	**Let's Build** Amy stayed home on Sunday. Today she is studying English. She's going to go to art class on Friday. When did Amy go to math class? When is Ben going to play with his friends? Asking and stating what people do and when **Let's Read** Welcome to Paul's Page!
Unit 8 Work and Play			
Let's Start Do you want to come? I can't. Sure! Making an invitation What's wrong? I have a cold. Asking and answering about illnesses	**Let's Learn** He/she likes/doesn't like to write e-mail. They like/don't like to watch sports on TV. What does he/she like to do? He/She likes to paint pictures. What do they like to do? They like to play badminton. Does he/she like to collect baseball cards? Yes, he/she does. / No, he/she doesn't. Do they like to watch sports on TV? Yes, they do. / No, they don't. Expressing likes and dislikes	**Let's Learn More** He/She has to wash the dishes. They have to clear the table. What does he/she have to do? He/she has to take out the trash. Asking and stating what someone has to do	**Let's Build** Talking about wants, needs, and likes **Let's Read** What Are You Like? Quiz
Units 7–8 Listen and Review		**Let's Read About Chris and Cindy Part Four**	

Word List

A

4
4
ittle more 71
lot 9
bout 20
dventures 73
ter 59
ternoon 58
go 2
rplane 19
l 34
ways 27
merican 63
musement park 44
n 9
nd 9
nimals 27
ny 6
nything 56
nywhere 47
pple 26
rchitect 22
re 56
rm 8
round 24
rt class 62
sked 37
stronaut 9
t 27
te 6
ugust 2
unt 2
ustralia 45
way 53

B

ackpacking 58
ad 32
adminton 66
ag 30
angs 48
arber shop 60
aseball 14
aseball cap 50
aseball cards 66
aseball game 40
at 14
e 20
each 12
eard 48
ears 34
eautiful 47
eauty salon 60
ecause 64
efore 7
est 28
etter 32
icycle 14
ig 19
igger 30
iggest 30
irthday 2
lack 47
lank 73
lond 48
louse 50
lue 30
oard game 40
boat 24
book 16
books 58
bored 39
borrow 58
bottle 30
box 30
boy 43
break 6
breakfast 9
bridge 42
broke 6
brother 49
brown 48
brush (v) 53
bucket 14
build 24
build a house 19
but 19

C

cake 32
call 65
came 7
camel 73
camera 13
can 17
candles 9
car 24
Carlsbad Caverns 73
carpet 68
castle 55
cave 55
cell phone 6
checked 51
cheetah 34
chocolate 6
chopsticks 26
clear the table 68
climb 24
climb a mountain 24
clue 19
coin 34
cold (adj) 10
cold (n) 65
collect 66
come on 21
cook (n) 33
cook (v) 26
cook dinner 26
cool 11
cough 65
cousin 47
crocodile 45
curly 48

D

dad 47
dance 21
dancer 21
dark 55
date 2
day 7
delivery person 22
dentist 65
department store 60
desert 55
design 24
did 5
didn't 2
different 53
dinner 26
dishes 68
do 5
doctor 65
does 23
doesn't 22
dog 26
doing 52
dolphins 27
don't 10
down 42
download 40
drank 4
drink 4
drive 24
drive a car 24
drives 27
drug store 60
dry the dishes 68
duck 35
DVD 58

E

earache 65
easier 28
easy 28
easygoing 71
eat 6
eating 52
Egypt 37
elephants 34
else 13
e-mail 66
embarassed 39
English 26
ever 34
everyone 46
excited 10
eyes 46

F

falcon 35
family 63
fast 35
faster 34
fastest 34
father 2
favorite 28
fed 45
feed 26
feed the dog 68
feeds 27
feel better 64
fever 65
fifteenth (15th) 3
fight 34
find 6
fingerprint 53
fire engine 34
first 7
fishing 15
fishing rod 14
flashlight 12
flew 4
flight attendant 22
fly 4
foggy 11
for 19
found 6
fourteen (14) 56
french fries 44
Friday 62
friend 49
fun 9

G

game 40
geography 29
get 6
gift shop 60
girl 43
glad 73
glass 17
glasses 50
go 4
go horseback riding 57
go on vacation 58
go shopping 57
going 3
good 32
good luck 56
got 6
grandfather 47
grandma 47
grandmother 47
grandpa 47
grandparents 40
gray 48
great 9
Great Pyramid 37
green 30

H

had 4
hair 46
hairbrush 34
hands 53
happened 6
Happy birthday! 2
hard 28
harder 37
hat 12
have 4
have fun 64
have to do 69
he 4
headache 65
heavier 31
heaviest 31
heavy 31
held 45
helmet 14
help 27
her 46
here 37
here's 55
he's 12
hiking 15
hill 42
hills 57
his 6
history 29
hold 45
holding 19
home 9
home stay 63
homework 26
hope 56
horse 35
hospital 27
hot 11
hot chocolate 4
house 24
how 9
humid 11
hurry 38

I

I 2
ice hockey 56
idea 21
Iguazu Falls 55
I'm 10
in 7
in front of 19
in the air 35
in water 35
indoors 17
inside 17
interested 39
into 42
is 2
isn't 10
it 7
it's 2

J

jackets 10
jeans 51
July 58
jump rope 34

K

kangaroo 45
key 34
kids 37
kite 4
know 2
koala 45

L

last week 41
last year 41
let's 21
letter 58
library 16
lift 53
light 31
lighter 31
lightest 31
lights 17
like 10
like to do 69
likes 27
lions 34
listen to 26
literature 29
live 35
long 31
longer 31
longest 31
look at 35
look like 49
looking for 46
lose 6
lost 6
lot 9
lotion 53

M

magic trick 21
make 39
many 35
March 37
math 66
matter 38
May 37
maybe 38
mom 28
Monday 65
month 37
morning 39
movies 50
music 68
music player 14
my 3

N

names 63
near 55
New Orleans 51
news reporter 21
next 19
next week 58
nice 29
no 10
no one 46
no problem! 38
not 11
novel 58
now 38
nurse 27

O

of 9
oh! 2
OK 46
old 56
older 49
on 2
on land 35
only 35
onto 17
or 14
orange 30
other 35
our 10
out of 42
over 42
over there 46

P

P.E. (physical education) 29
paint 66
paint pictures 66
pancakes 9
paper 11
paper clip 34
parents 9
park 64
party 4
pencil 31
people 27
piano 26
pictures 26
pie 32
piece 53
piece of paper 53
piece of tape 53
ping-pong 26
pink 51
pizza 16
place 55
plaid 51
plant 56
plant flowers 57
play (n) 57
play (v) 14
play ice hockey 57
play softball 57
polar bears 34
police car 34
polka-dot 51
pond 42
pony tail 48
pop idol 22
powder 53
practice 26
practice the piano 26
practiced 40
present 6
probably 14
purple 51
put 17

R

race 6
radio 40
rain (v) 10
rainbow 17
read 19
really 10
really? 2
red 46
rent 58
reptile 45
restaurant 9
rhinos 34
ribbon 34
rich 20
ride 15
rides 27
right over there 47
roller coaster 38
ruler 34
run 26
runner 33

S

said 19
sail (v) 24
sail a boat 24
sailfish 35
sailing (n) 45
same 53
sand 19
sandals 50
sandwich 44
Saturday 59
save 71
says 11
scared 45
school trip 10
science 28
scientist 21
scrapbook 73
second (2nd) 17
see 17
see a play 57
see you soon! 45
serious 71
she 4
she's 12
shine 17
shirt 51
shopping 57
short 31
shorter 31
shortest 31
shorts 51
should 10
shouldn't 12
show (n) 38
sick 64
sing 21
singer 20
sister 27
ski 57
skis 57
sleeping bag 12
slightly 17
slow 35
small 17
smaller 30
smallest 30
sneakers 50
snow (n) 57
snow (v) 11
so 10
soccer player 33
softball 56
some 6
someday 27
someone 46
sore throat 65
Space Center 9
speak 26
speed 35
spend 71
sports 66
standing 73
stay 56
stay home 56
stayed 63
stomachache 64
store 4
straight 48
striped 51
study 26
studying 62
subject 28
suit 50
summer 58
summer vacation 44
Sunday 8
sunglasses 12
sunscreen 12
supermarket 60
sure 15
surf the Internet 66
surprise 47
surprised 39
swan 35
swim 26
swimmer 33
swimming (n) 15
swimsuit 12

T

table 68
take 4
take out the trash 68
take pictures 26
talk 26
tall 47
tape 53
tea 65
teacher 29
telephone 26
tennis 15
tennis ball 14
tennis racket 14
tent 12
test 4
than 28
thanks 38
that 2
that's 20
the 2
their 40
them 27
then 9
there's 19
they 6
they're 15
think 10
third (3rd) 2
this 9
three (3) 2
through 42
tie 50
tilt 17
to 4
today 2
today's 2
tomorrow 3
tonight 58
too 6
took 4
toothache 65
touch 53
tour 9
tour guide 22
towel 12
train 27
trainer 27
trash 68
travel 24
treasure 55
treasure hunt 19
triangle 19
trip 8
truck driver 22
T-shirt 52
Tuesday 3
tunnel 42
turn off 17
turtle 26
TV 26
TV show 21
twentieth (20th) 3
twenty-eighth (28th) 8
twenty-first (21st) 2
twenty-second (22nd) 3
two (2) 63

U

umbrellas 10
uncle 37, 47
under 42
underground 55
United States 63
up 17
use 26

V

vacuum 68
vacuum the carpet 68
very 39
vest 50
video game 24
violin 40
visit 40
volunteer 27

W

wait 38
waiting in line 38
walk 26
wall 17
want 20
wants 16
warm 11
was 2
wash 68
wash the dishes 68
watch (v) 26
watch TV 26
water 17
waterfall 37
we 7
wearing 50
weather 10
weatherman 11
weekend 56
weeks 2
weeks ago 41
well 65
went 4
we're 19
wet 55
whale 35
what 5
what happened? 7
what's 2
what's the matter? 47
what's wrong? 64
when 2
when's 2
where 19
where's 16
which 28
white 51
who 9
who's 33
why 28
why not 64
wildlife park 45
win 6
window 6
with 27
woman 52
won 6
woods 42
work 27
works 27
world 24
worried 39
worse 32
worst 32
wow 20
write 66
write e-mail 66
writer 21

Y

yeah 19
year 9
yellow 51
yes 10
yesterday 2
you 17
younger 47
your 2
you're 17

Z

zoo 27